- Trace the dotted lines from top to botto

- Trace the dotted lines from left to right

Writing the Alphabet

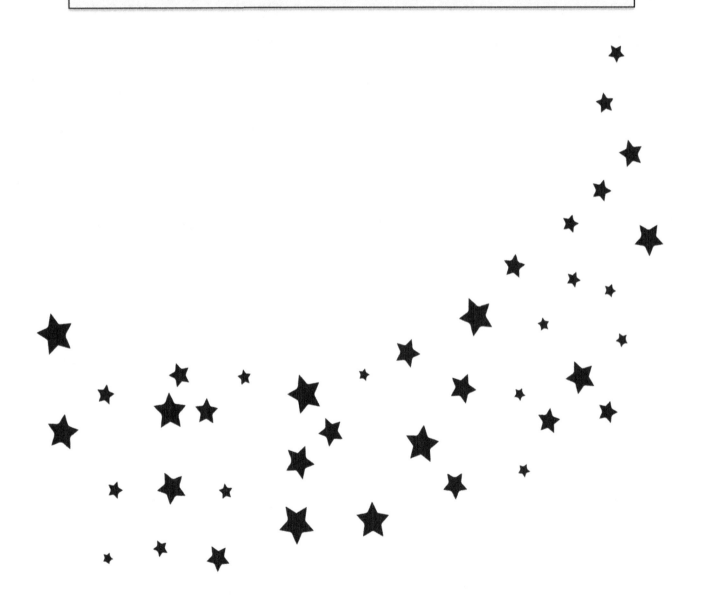

C IS FOR CLOUD

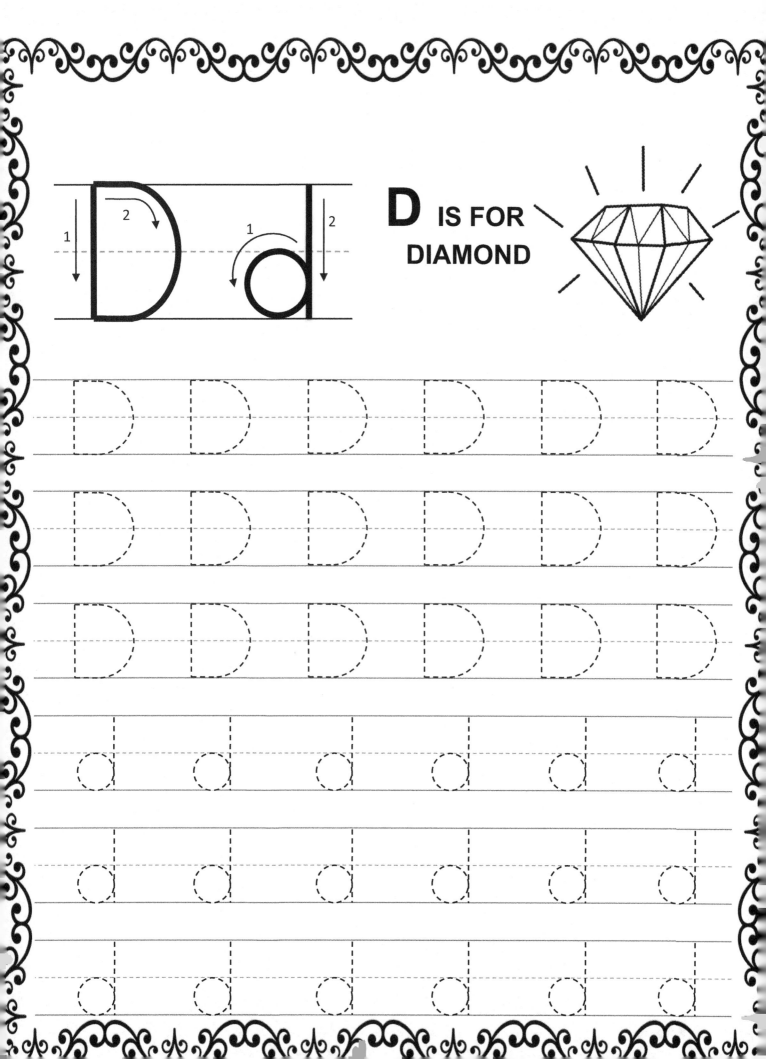

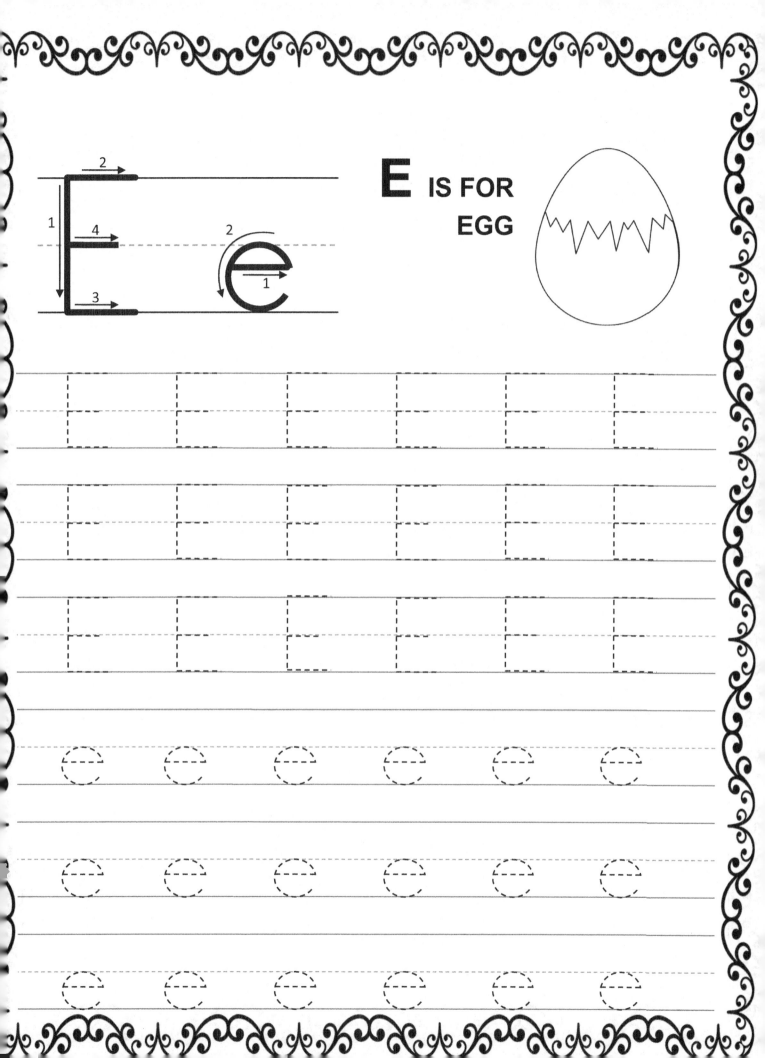

F IS FOR FLOWER

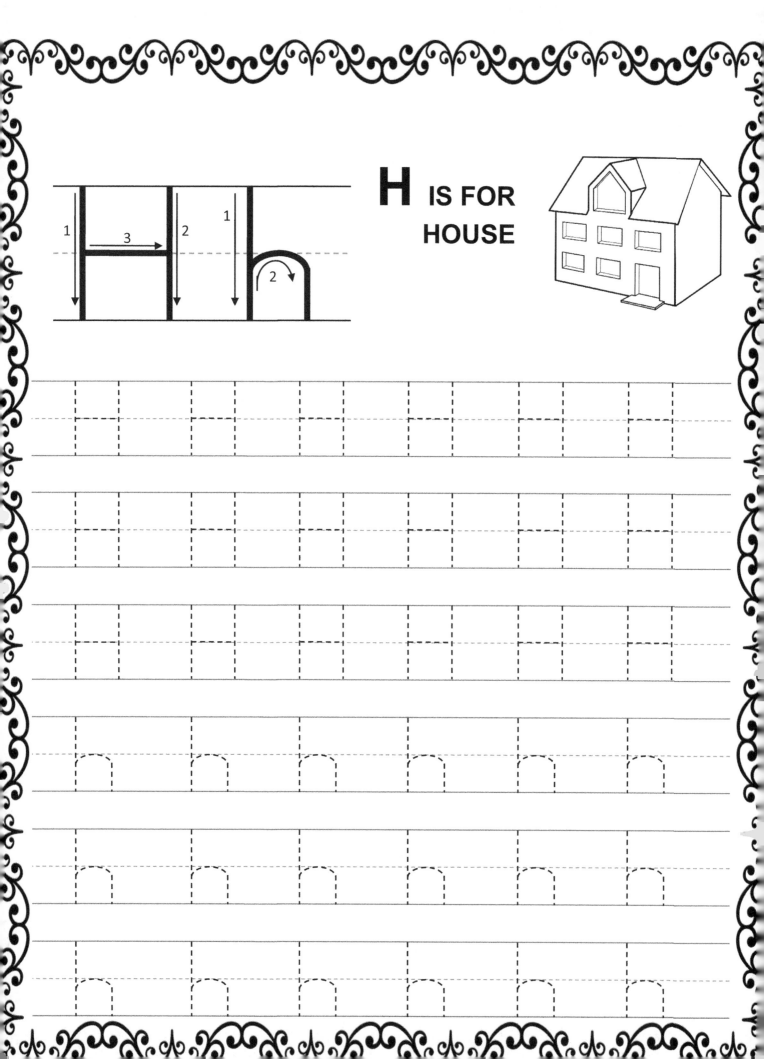

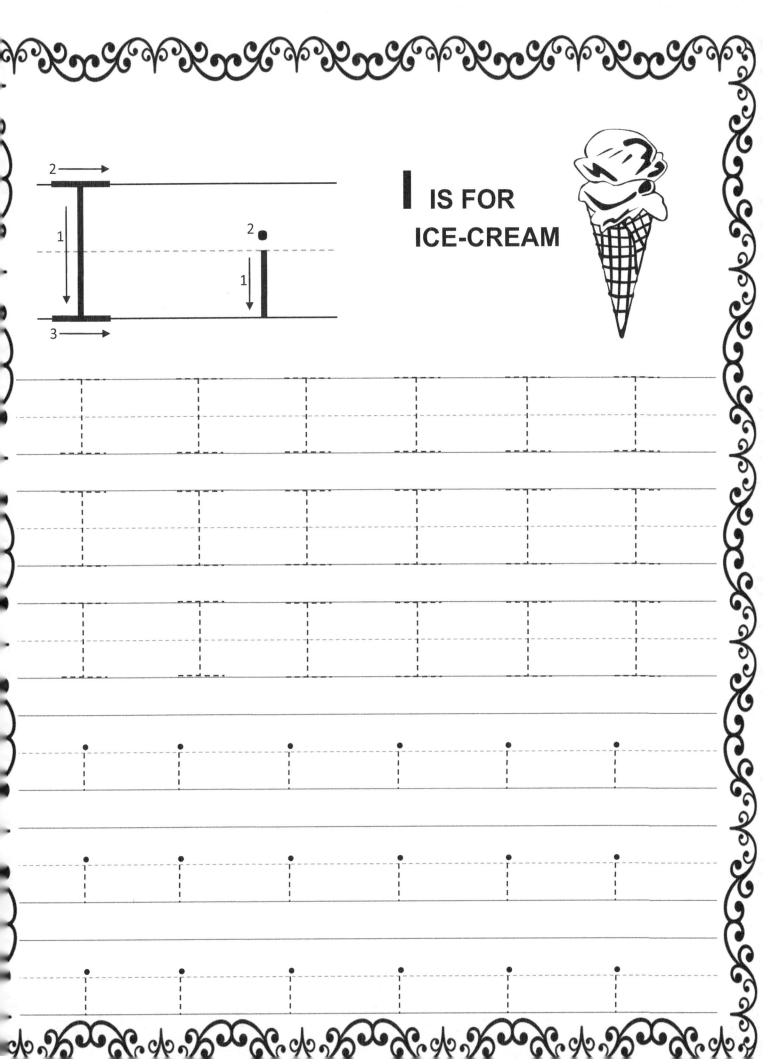

J IS FOR JUICE

L IS FOR LADDER

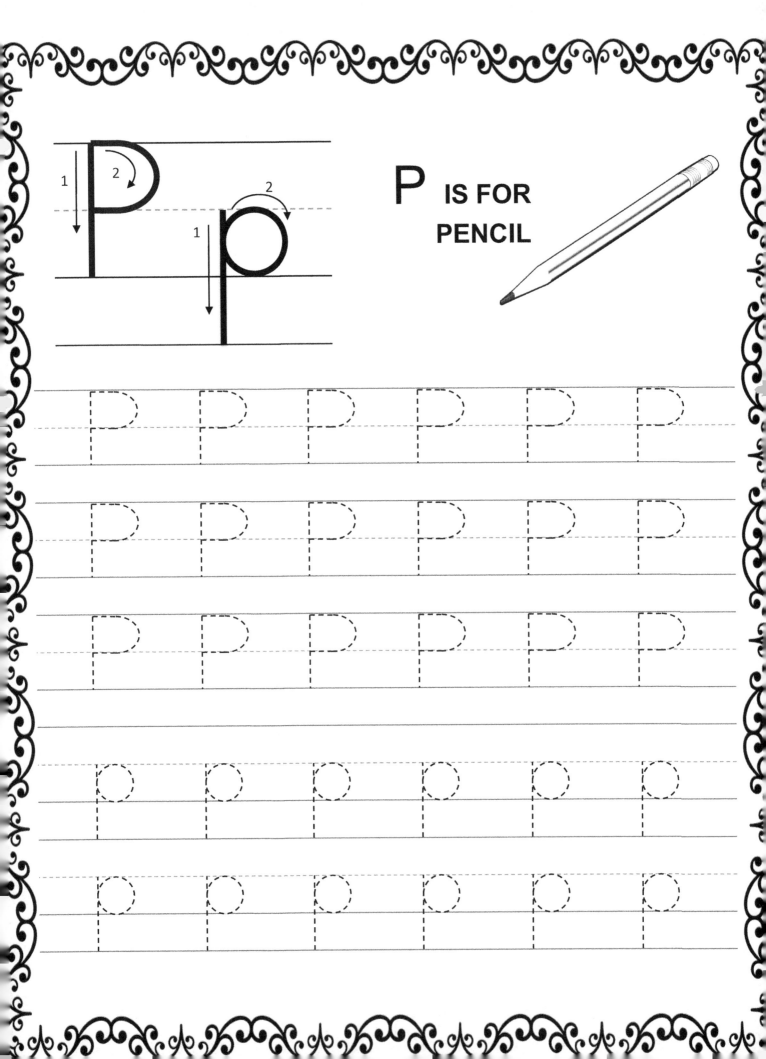

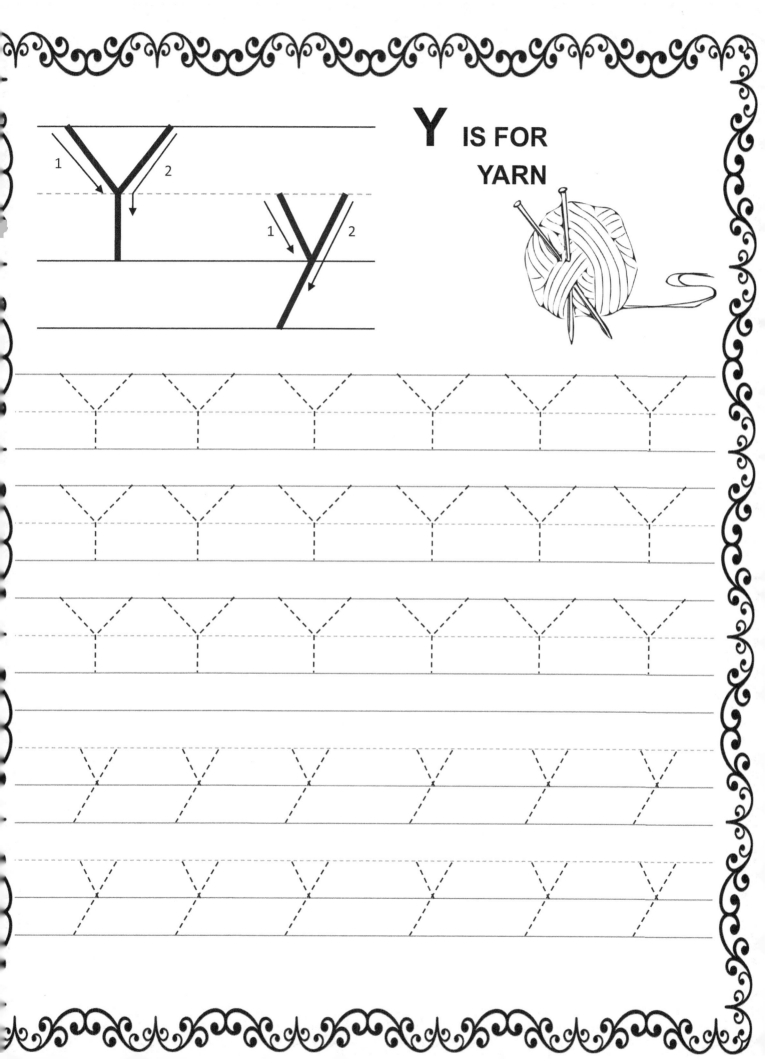

Z IS FOR ZIP

Writing sight words

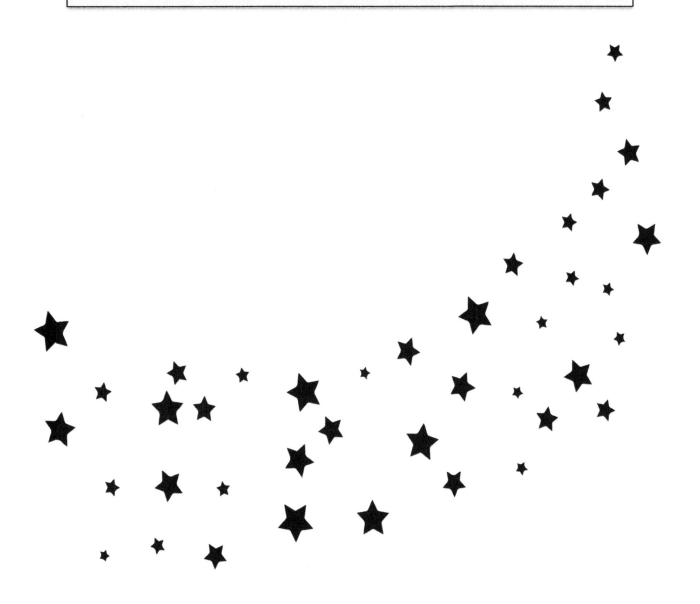

am am am am

am

an an an an an

an

And And And And

And And

at at at at at at

at

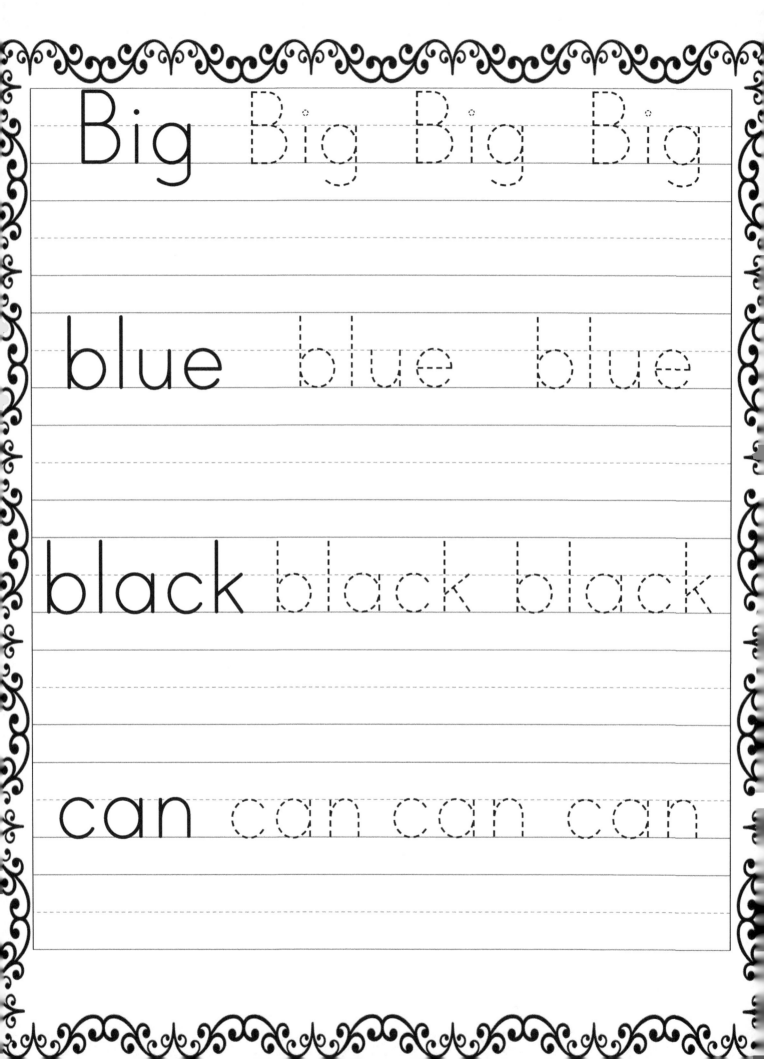

put put put put

queen queen

Quiet Quiet Quiet

red red red red

Run Run Run Run

ran ran ran ran

Ride Ride Ride

Round Round

said said said

See See See See

saw saw saw saw

she she she she

you you you you

Yellow Yellow

yes yes yes yes

Your Your Your

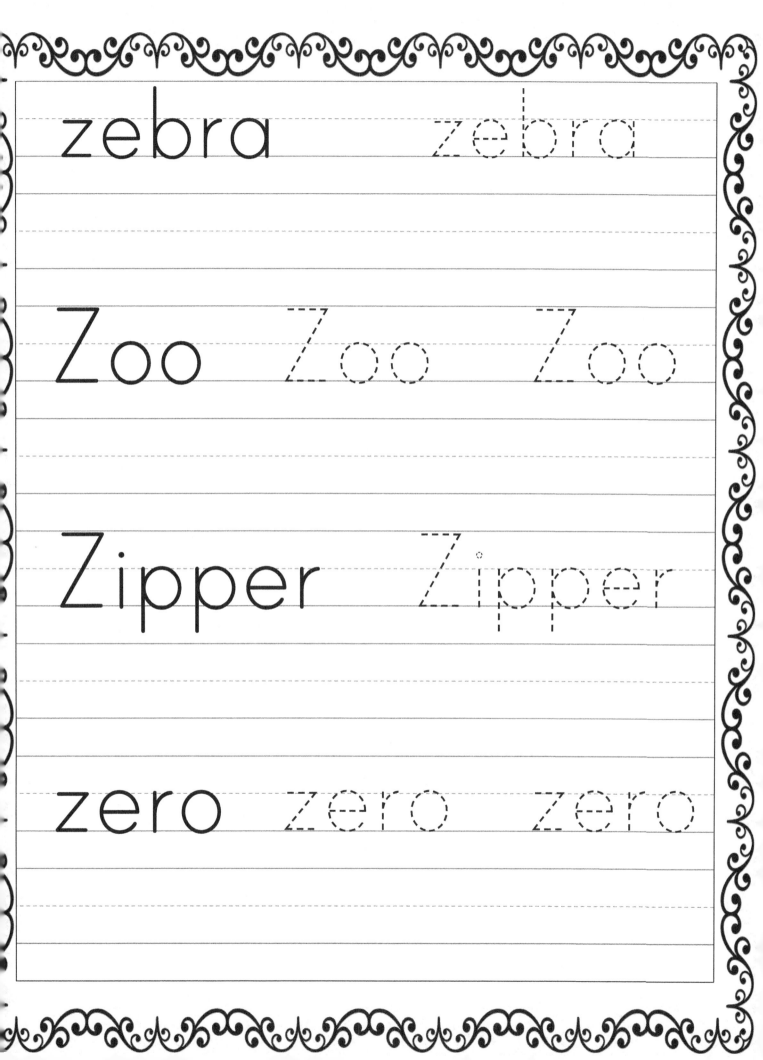

Made in the USA
Middletown, DE
24 September 2020